Childish Behaviour Childish Peoples

Lindsey Powell

BookLeaf Publishing

Childish Poems for Childish Peoples © 2022
Lindsey Powell

All rights reserved.

No part of this publication may be reproduced, stored in a retrieval system, or transmitted, in any form or by any means, electronic, mechanical, photocopying, recording or otherwise, without the prior written permission of the presenters.

Lindsey Powell asserts the moral right to be identified as author of this work.

Presentation by *BookLeaf Publishing*

Web: www.bookleafpub.com

E-mail: info@bookleafpub.com

ISBN: 9789357618571

First edition 2022

I would like to dedicate this book to my daughters, Hattie-Bear and Bertie-Boo. Thank you for teaching me to be silly and to see the best in the little things. I love your sparkle, your fierceness and your relentless happiness. I love you both.

ACKNOWLEDGEMENT

Many thanks to my husband for always believing in me and supporting my crazy ideas, to my parents for always supporting my academic endeavours and of course to my family for being wonderfully weird enough to inspire these stories! You are all my very favourite peoples.

PREFACE

My hope is that sharing these poems together as a family will help grown-ups to grow back down and enjoy life the spontaneous and pure way children still can. The book is about taking little moments and ideals in life and then making the happiest memories possible, even when life can be challenging or confusing. The stories show a range of relatable characters to set an achievable example of personal growth and acceptance.

The Pea In The Sea

Somewhere on a dinner plate was a very unhappy little pea,
Who didn't want to be squashed between potatoes, carrots and gravy.
In fact she dreamed of adventures and being truly free,
Yes, she desperately longed to travel and visit the sea.

The pea made up her mind and summoned all her might,
She rocked and she rolled, until the little pea took flight.
She rolled off the dinner plate and far off to the right,
Then the pea dropped off the table, safe out of sight.

As the pea wondered what to do, she saw a roller skate,
Dropped by the children when they were running late.
She swiftly climbed aboard and thought "Well great,
This will take me to the sea, it must have been fate".

She skated out of the house and down the garden path,
"Where's the sea" wondered the pea "I really need a map."
Then she smelled the sea air, all salty not like a bath,
And she skated on forwards unaware of the terrible trap.

Just then the seagull that soared above swooped quickly down,
He snatched the pea up in his claws and flew high off the ground,
The little pea trembled, feeling helpless, green and round,
But then she saw the sea and heard the waves crashing sound.

Suddenly the seagull swooped and loosened his grip,
Out of his claws the green pea did begin to slip.
She hurtled swiftly to the floor, on a one-way trip,
And luckily, she landed softly in a cone of chips.

"Who are you?" The chips did gasp and moan.
Looking cross the chips all said "Hey this is our cone,
"If you want a plate go and get your own!"
Suddenly, the little pea felt very very alone.

"Oh dear" cried the pea "It was an accident you see,
I'm not stopping I'm off to see the sea, please excuse me."
"A pea in the sea" the chips all laughed loudly,
"We'll help you, this we would really love to see!"

So a chip flicked the pea who darted through the air,

She carried on her crazy journey to who knows where.
But she splashed in an ice cream of a girl with curly hair,
Who had no idea that the little green pea was even there.

The little girl skipped down the promenade and across the sand,
Smiling as she wandered happily with ice cream in hand.
The pea was so pleased to see the water meets the land,
Finally, she reached the sea just ask the little pea had planned.

Now the pea hopped off the ice cream on to a pea-size boat,
Made of slimy seaweed so the little green pea could float.
She waved bye to the ice cream and tried not to gloat,
But she had made it to the sea after all the others had joked.

And so the little green pea was finally in the sea,
She bobbed along on the waves very happily.
She aimed for the horizon as far as she could see,
Now dreaming more adventures for a green sea pea.

Hodge the Veg-Hog

Hodge was a little hedgehog who lived in a country hedge,
At teatime he ate all of his meat but never his veg.
Mummy smiled "Try these peas please Hodge,
Just treats and meats will make your tummy podge.
Or have some carrots" said Mummy "they are very nice."
"No THANK YOU" moaned Hodge and shook his head twice.
So Mummy and Hodge found a deal they could make,
If he ate three of her veggies she would bake him a cake.

On Monday Hodge saw the peas and thought "Of course,
I'll cover them all in red tomato sauce."
He tried and he tried to open up wide,
And swallow the peas deep down inside.
But now the peas looked too mushy and too gushy,
"Sorry, no cake today Hodge" Mummy replied.

On Tuesday Hodge saw the broccoli and looked to his mother,
Then he smothered it in enough gravy to cover.
He tried and he tried to open up wide,
And swallow the broccoli deep down inside.
But now the broccoli looked too funny and too runny,
"Sorry, no cake today Hodge" Mummy replied.

On Wednesday Hodge saw the carrots and his hopes were almost trashed,
So he squashed them with a fork until they were matched.
He tried and he tried to open up wide,
And swallow the carrots deep down inside.
But now the carrots look too sloppy and two gloppy
"Sorry, no cake today Hodge" Mummy replied.
Both Mummy and Hodge knew it was not going great,
"But tomorrow" Hodge promised "I'll empty my plate."
On Thursday Hodge pretended that the peas were chocolate drops,
Then he closed his eyes, and he scoffed up the lot.
On Friday Hodge pretended that the broccoli was really ice cream,
Then he closed his eyes, and it went down like a dream.
On Saturday Hodge pretended that the carrots were sweets,
Then he closed his eyes and ate all his veg not just meats.
"Well done Hodge" cried mummy "I am so proud of you"
"Yay, I ate all my veggies" beamed Hodge "and I liked them all too."

On Sunday Hodge really looked forward to their family lunch,
He'd eat all three veggies today, that was his hunch.

Then mummy brought out a GIANT chocolate cake for the table,
"When you've eaten your veggies a slice is for you if you're able!"
Hodge ate all his carrots, all his broccoli and all his peas.
He was almost ready for cake but then he smiled "More please!"
"Of course dear" gleamed mummy "there's plenty more meat Hodge"
"No thanks mummy" Hodge joked "because I'm now a veg hog!!!"

Fussy Flo the Flamingo

Flo was a very fussy Flamingo, who liked things to be just so.
She knew what she liked, and what she did not.
And once she made-up her mind, she never forgot.
Flo said what she meant and meant what she said.
Yes, she always had a clever idea in her head.

Flo was never too quiet; she used her voice.
And always believed that she had a choice.
Her Mommy loved that her spirit was strong.
Yet, flow knew how to admit she was wrong.
She certainly knew how to speak her mind,
But Mommy still wanted to help her be kind.

At sports day Mommy said, "Even if you don't win the race,
just do your best Flo and keep a smile on your face."
Mommy would tell her to say "Well done" to her friends,
But to never give up and to try and try again.

When Flo argued with her sister because they couldn't share,
Mommy explain to them both "Come on now be fair.
Have three goals each and then you can swap,
You can both play nicely without any strops."

Mommy said "Words have power to hurt peoples' feelings,
Choose your words wisely and remember their meanings.
When you feel cross, just stop and think twice,
Before you say something that's not very nice."

One day out with Mummy, Flo was fussy at the shops,
She set her heart on having a pretty blue top.
"Sorry Flo we can't have it now" said Mommy,
"You'll have to wait and save up the money."

Flo really wanted the top, and she wanted it bad,
She didn't want to leave it there and to become sad.
Then she thought of Mommy's words, about how words can hurt.

"You're right Mommy" she smiled "I'll save up for my blue shirt."

"It's OK to be fussy" Mommy said "if you still try to be kind,
Just say what you think nicely and keep others in mind."
Then mommy said gently as she looked down and smiled
"I'm proud of how hard you try Flo, all of the while."
"Oh Mommy you're so lovely" said Flo "and so very clever."
"Thanks for teaching me to be kind, you're the best Mommy ever."

Jenny the Giraffe

Jenny the giraffe was very, very tall,
In fact she wasn't small, not at all, she said,
Like all giraffes she has a long neck and long legs.
With spiky black hair, and horns on her head.
Jenny lives on the great grass plains,
By the watering hole sandy shore,
Along with her good friends the lions,
the elephants, the hippos and more.

Unlike the black and white zebras,
Giraffes have spots instead of stripes.
Each one has their own unique pattern,
So they don't ever look alike.
Jenny loves to eat the juiciest leaves,
At the top of the trees,
Where her head is so high,
She can see for miles in the breeze

With her family Jenny lives,
On the continent of Africa running free.
But you can see other giraffes,
In an enclosure at a zoo or sanctuary.
Because giraffes are endangered,
Now there aren't very many,
So we must save them together,
For our children to see any.

Debra the Fashion Zebra

Debra the zebra liked to wear tights,
So she had fashion choices other than stripes.
She had spotty ones and dotty ones,
All crazy colours, orange and blue,
Thick fluffy ones and thin silky ones,
Bobbly old pairs and some brand new.
Debra was sick of plain black and white,
She wanted colour and patterns in her life.
She started a fashion line of spangly tights,
All designed by her each day and night.
There were pinks and green and reds,
And furry ones with swirls,
Big ones for fancy ladies,
And teeny tiny ones for baby girls.
She dreamed up her designs before she went to bed,
And Debra sketch designs in a book to get them out of her head.
Soon everyone was buying them,
And her tights were in every shop,
So no zebra had to be boring,
If they wanted a fashion swap.
Debra was a happy zebra now in her clothes,
She loved all the patterns and colours she chose.

Boo the Button Pusher

Boo loved pushing a button that she shouldn't push,
She enjoyed smooshing things she shouldn't smoosh,
If there was a loose thread, she would pull it always,
She liked wearing odd socks except on Sundays,
Forever into mischief with a big cheeky grin,
With craziest ideas that will help her team win,
Boo was a terrible fidget and she liked to explore,
She'd lose things under the sofa and on the floor,
Always there to investigate a strange sounding noise,
And somehow manage to break some of her toys,
"Try to be gentle" her Daddy would say,
Boo would try of course but it was just her clumsy way,
She dropped things when she should hold tight,
Or went left when she meant to go right,
Boo would take a detour and talk to a friend,
She would investigate and notice more in the end,
Whatever needed testing she was the best one to do it,
And she loved discovering new ways to prove it,
Yes Boo could fidget and wriggle forever and ever,
But the experiences life gave her made her so very clever,
So push those giant shiny fidgety buttons for us Boo,
And tell us what you find out in the world when you do.

Nephew Nephew

Nephews are like your siblings but smaller you see,
And they haven't had to grow up so they are still silly.
Nephews like to play tricks and set lots of traps,
They tell silly jokes and do wiggle-butt slaps.
Nephews know a hundred different words for poop,
And can make muddy slime into globbedy goop.
Nephews always stay up late and get up super early,
They run around in circles until their brain is all whirly.
Nephews are covered in chocolate and have a cheeky smile,
They remember your stories even if it has been a while.
Nephews like to watch the TV with you the best,
Because you let them watch the scary films, unlike the rest.
Nephews love to tell you all about their computer game,
Even though you don't really care and it drives you insane.
Nephews like to go for adventures with you outside,
And find the best super-secret places to hide.
Nephews play funny music and sing random songs,
They like to tell you sometimes you're getting it wrong.
Nephews can be loud and funny and mega crazy,
And now they are getting older they become a bit lazy.
Nephews give great hugs and squeeze you tight,
But to get a goodbye kiss now is a real flight.
Nephews are my very favourite people it's true,
And I hope you realise nephews, how much I love you.

Aunt-tea

My Aunt-tea really really LOVES drinking tea,
Yes indeed she takes it very very seriously.
She'll drink a lovely cuppa all day and all night,
Once up a mountain and even on a flight.
She's got tea leaves and loads of weird teapots,
A hundred cups and mugs, she's got lots and lots.
My Aunt-tea likes tea when she's happy or sad,
She's got teacup earrings, she's completely tea-mad.
At work she always sorts a good mug of tea,
I actually think she could drink it professionally.
Tea is for the seaside and tea is for bed,
You could offer anything and she'd pick tea instead.
A nice cuppa to warm you after a soggy Autumn walk,
Or a pot of tea in the kitchen for a giggle and talk.
Aunt-tea especially loves a good afternoon tea,
Yes a fine China cup and cakes, oh how lovely!
And if I've got a problem Aunt-tea is always there,
We'll have a cuppa together, a chat and share.
Then I'll feel so much better almost immediately,
Aunt-tea says you can fix anything, with a nice up of tea.

My Uncle Is A Magical Badger

We're not sure how it happened,
It's a seriously spooky mystery.
But my uncle turned into a badger,
He just changed one night magically.
He has black and white fur,
With a stripe down his nose,
Uncle's got great big paws,
And sharp claws on his toes.
One crazy Saturday night out,
He drank a magical drink.
It must have been a witch's potion,
Or a sorcerer's spell we think.
Then next day he was hibernating,
And groaning with growls,
Uncle's eyes were now tiny,
And his face was all scowls.
When he emerged on the Sunday,
Finally from sleeping in his den.
We noticed he'd suddenly changed,
And we'd got a badger for an Uncle then.
Now he only comes out very late,
And stays up partying all night,
He tells us unbelievable stories of adventures,
Yeah he's crazy funny alright!
Having a magical badger for an Uncle,
Is loads of fun you see.
I never know what he'll do next,
Or where he'll take me.

The Professional Grandad

"I thought you'd retired" Grandma said,
As she looked at Grandad and shook her head.
"You're always tatting, you never sit still,
Have you working too hard those Grandkids will"
"Retired? You? Really Grandad?" I said,
As I thought of him, lazing about instead.
"Not quite" Grandad smiled "I've got so much to do,
Having the best time playing with you"
I thought about this all through the night,
We do lots of things together, Grandad was right.
We wander in the woods and climb tall trees,
Then splash in the stream and get muddy knees.
Grandad always let me watch the best TV,
And makes up stories with characters like me,
We collect wiggly sticks and jaggedy stones,
Pick up smooth feathers and spikey pinecones,
In the garden Grandad said he'll teach me all he knows,
Like planting acorns and helping them grow.
We make blanket forts with cushions and a sheet,
Then we have sleepovers together each week.
We get loads of snacks and pillows and my teddy,
And make spooky faces with torches when ready.
Grandma looks at the mess and her face spells trouble,
But when she looks at Grandad her smile doubles.
He's the head mischief maker now he's retired,
Until he falls asleep in the chair when he's tired.
 "I love being with you, retirement is not really so bad"
He smiles down "because now I'm a Professional grandad!"

Spangly Glam-ma

She's not your basic Grandma I'll have you all know,
Mine is actually a Glam-ma, everyone always says so.
"What on Earth's a Glam-ma!" I hear you exclaim,
Well, she's like a Nanny but a bit extra and not plain.
My Glam-ma has 70 dresses she made of all different fabrics,
And a hundred more fancy dress ones stuffed up in the attic.
Then there's the shoes, yes the shoes, the glorious shoes,
In pinks and purples and blues or any colour you'd chose.
Poor grandad can't even lift the suitcases to go on a flight,
But Glam-ma says "I'm 73 now and I'll never packed light."
Of course, then you need sparkly bracelets and spangly beads,
Glam-ma is indeed the best at matching all her accessories.
Don't forget the coordinating gloves and delicate scarves,
Yes Glam-ma is always well turned out,
she doesn't do it by halves.
Handbags are super important to carry all of your bits,
Like pretty hankies, a flowery umbrella and bright lipsticks.
But my favourite outfit is when she wears all ruby red,
Because it's her very favourite colour she once said.
Yet for all Glam-ma's amazing fashions and style,
Her best feature is truly her lovely, lovely smile.

Grampy The Nanny

Grampy wasn't like all the other nannies,
For a start he had a great big bushy beard,
No, the other nannies didn't have hairy faces,
Because that would just be super weird.

Grampy always told the funniest stories and tales,
About a magical badger and a fluffy bunny,
They lived in a faraway woodland together,
Yes, Grampy 's imagination was really rather funny.

All the other nannies fed you vegetables,
But my Grampy definitely did not.
He'd get a giant loaf of bread,
And toast up the whole lot.

Grampy taught you to squeeze the biscuits,
Into your mouth all in one go.
But every other one of the nannies,
Would always just shout NOOOOOO!

Nannies are supposed to wear dresses,
With flowers and lots of big beads.
But Grampy always wore dark green,
To camouflage amongst the bushes and trees.

Grampy was different to all the other nannies,
In a lot of strange and silly ways.
For a start all the nannies had handbags,
That they carried around all day.

In their bags the nannies kept stuff,
Like tissues, a purse and a red lipstick
But Grampy collected random pockets full,

Of pinecones, feathers and a catapult stick.

Yet when it came to the important things,
Grampy and the nannies were all just as good.
Because Grampy always came to see me,
Just as often as he could.

My Grampy always says "I love you"
And gives me the squeeziest hug.
Then he sings me to sleep,
And he tucks me in real snug.

Vigi-Gran-te And The Ability Scooter

Well yeah, I'm sure you've got a really nice Nanny,
But mine is special because she's a Vigi-Gran-te,
Yes, she does crochet and crafts like all the others,
But at night she fights crime as a dark vigilante.
Now she patrols the streets on her Ability Scooter,
Looking for baddies who need to be put right,
Her scooter has tones of special secret gadgets,
Llike a wrinkly superhero, Vigigrante wins every fight.
She uses the scooter's super nabber grabber,
When finding naughty pests who drop litter around,
Vigigrante's grabber makes them bin all the rubbish,
And scares them to drop any more on the ground.
Like an aged agent of justice, she goes out to patrol,
And spies on the baddies who double park their cars,
If they block the pavement for wheelchairs,
She'd clamp all their wheels with big heavy bars.
Also, the Ability Scooter had the LOUDEST horn,
If Vigigrante ever saw evil burglars lurk,
She's sound her monstrous horn to scare them,
And as they ran away she'd triumphantly smirk.
Vigigrante is mega fast at her at her top speed,
She would always beat the baddies in a race,
And the Ability Scooter was super stealthy too,
It could sneak in without a single trace.
But thinking about Vigigrante a little bit more,
Not all her abilities come from the chair,
Yes, Vigigrante has many true talents,
That have always been there.
Like all crimefighters should truly be,
She's kind and brave, thoughtful and honest,
And even without the Ability Scooter,
Vigigrante is talented and creative, cheeky and modest.

The Ability Scooter helps her fight crime no doubt,
Yet the real magic was there inside before,
The scooter just makes it so much easier,
For Vigigrante to go out cruising on tour.
When she needs a rest from keeping justice,
She can sleep in very late,
And do some more crocheting and crafts,
With me, her little best mate.

The 49-Year-Old Boy

You don't really have to grow up,
Its just something people want you to do.
You could choose to be a kid forever,
If that's what best suits you.

I know a boy who is 49 years old,
He never wanted to grow up.
So he said to all the other adults,
"I won't you know, it's just tough luck".

The big boy loves his trains tracks,
And he still collects motor cars.
He would read superhero comic books,
And watch movies about the stars.

The boy would always ask for toys,
Each Christmas for 49 years.
He would still laugh at silly jokes,
And he'd laugh himself to tears.

Some of the other sad grown-ups,
Wondered if he could be serious again.
"Why would I?" the boy would say,
As he was always happier than them.

Life needs a little bit of magic,
And a healthy dose of childish whimsy,
There's plenty of time for mortgages,
And watching the boring news on TV.

He loved fantasy stories from books and films,
With adventures and wonderous schemes.
The big boy saw lots of possibilities,

And didn't give up his hopes and dreams.

Well then kids, if the choice was yours,
A grown up or a kid would you be?
And the big boy, well he turns 50 soon,
But he'll still be a child believe me.

Remember Farts Are Funny

Why don't parents still find farts funny?
Why are they always talking about chores and money?
Why can't they jump in puddles with a big, massive squelch?
Why don't they still laugh at a booming rumbling belch?
Why are parents always on about going to boring work?
Why do they say in the mornings their whole body hurts?
Why don't parents blow raspberries and tickle under my arms?
Why don't they stay up late and turn off their daily alarms?
Why do parents say that you always have to go to school?
Why do they shout put your shoes on and make up the rules?
Why can't they be like kids and enjoy making a big mess?
Why can't we have fun and get muddy in a posh dress?
Why should kids stop finding poop jokes super funny?
Why wouldn't they laugh about a snotty nose that's runny?
Why can't parents have fun and break every rule?
Why can't they be free like children and covered in drool?
Why don't we make a blanket fort with the cushions on the settee?
Why shouldn't you stay at home all day and play with me?
Why do parents say you have to eat veggies and a healthy diet?
Why do we need to behave, do our homework and be quiet?
Why can't parents just be silly and funny and crazy?
Why can't they sit with us, snuggle up and be lazy?
Why did parents forget what it's like to be a kid?
Why do I find it so sad that they did?
Let the kids teach the parents how to grow back down,
Let's talk in weird voices and all mess around,
Let's jump on the bed in our underpants,
Let's turn up the music and do the wiggle-bum dance,
Let's have ice cream for dinner and cake before bed,
Let's sing silly songs and stand on our head,
Let's enjoy being together outside when it's sunny,
Let the kids help parents remember why farts are still funny.

Stinkit The Stinkiest Dog.

Some dogs are very clever, some are super funny,
Some are handsome dogs, worth lots of money.
Big dogs are great guard dogs, keeping things safe,
While the best lap dogs, the cute little ones make.
Special dogs are guide dogs, helping people each day,
They are very well trained and show them the way.
The police dogs can sniff for drugs and bag guys,
Energetic sheep dogs heard sheep and are very wise.
But Stinkit wasn't like other dogs in so many ways,
He snored all night and slept through his days.
There were no special tricks that Stinkit could do,
He couldn't speak or spin or catch a ball too.
Stickit's one unique power was unfortunately bad,
Sometimes it made him feel a little sad.
Everyone has a talent at which they're the best,
And poor Stinkit's was pumping like a stinky stinky pest.
He could clear a room within minutes on a bad day,
"Oh Stinkit, how could you?" they'd cough and say.
Yet Stinkit had a cute little face and a waggedy tail,
But people only remembered the smell I'm afraid.
So Stinkit got a little sad and decided to run away,
He thought his family would be happier that way.
While he was missing his family were heartbroken for sure,
Despite the smell they loved him, because his heart was pure.
They search for him everywhere to bring Stinkit home,
And cried when they thought of him scared and alone.
Stinkit regretted leaving his family; he was lost and afraid,
He wished he'd talked to them, hating the decision he made.
He'd be a good dog, he'd promise to get back on track,
Stinkit would do anything to get his hooman family back.
As they looked for him they began to lose all hope,
Where could he be, it was getting dark, this was no joke.
And then suddenly a terrible, awful, lingering smell did appear,
Everyone cheered loudly because they knew that Stinkit was near.
"Oh Stinkit we've found you, you're such a good stinky boy"
The family snuggled him up and all smiled with pure joy.

For once in his life, Stinkit was proud of his smell,
And he knew his family truly loved him, of he could tell.
Nobody is ever perfect, which Stinkit now knows,
But we are who we are, and that's just how life goes.

The Pixilettes of Thistledown Town

There's a whole other world that you never realised was there,
A tiny world of tiny people hidden secretly in the woodland trees,
You never knew they existed but, in the forest, here they are,
Living in houses made of mushrooms and riding bumble bees.
These magical little people have lived there a thousand years,
They have built a wonderful little place with nature all around,
Safe away from humans and hidden, the Pixilettes do live,
In a magical place with spiky thistles called Thistledown Town.
Pixilettes are tiny folk no bigger than a growing rose bud,
They have pointy little ears and luscious curly hair,
Their clothes are made from thistle flowers and ivy leaves,
Yet they never will wear any shoes, their feet are always bare.
Thistledown Town is deep in the woods hidden well away,
The thorns of the thistles protect them from troubles outside,
And the Pixilettes are so small they become invisible to humans,
So they can carry on their business and never have to hide.
Two of the younglettes were out one day exploring very far,
Little Henriella and Robertina were playing in the happily wood,
But they forgot about the pathways when chasing butterflies,
The girls went much further than they promised mother they would.
The Pixilettes didn't notice they were lost for a good long while,
Because they were too excited about what they had found,
The looked up and saw big girl, a real-life human girl was there,
Oh my, the younglettes stumbled into a big giant human town.
The place was magical and alive with busy people busy-ing about,
The two Pixilettes loved the delicious food smells and bright light,
Henriella and Robertina watch a big human girl singing with glee,
They followed her home not realising it had now turned to night.
The younglettes watch the girl with her human family,
They were so much like any Pixilettes with a mom and a dad,
They had dinner, read books and got ready for bedtime like us,
Now the girls wondered if humans really were all that bad.
They'd stay a while and watch her to make up their mind,
So upstairs to the bedroom Henriella and Robertina did creep,
To find out more about the big girl and who she really was,
The Pixilettes explored the house and watched her sleep.
The big girl's room was amazing and full of wonderous toys,
She had the most beautiful dolls and squashiest teddy,
The younglettes decided the human girl was good and kind-hearted,
And they wanted to stay but they'd been gone too long already.
Henriella and Robertina crept out of the house to the garden,

The leaves and the flowers were swaying in the night breeze,
Now the Pixilettes were worried how they'd ever get home,
When suddenly they heard to buzzing of the bumble bees.
The kind bees gave them a ride home on their fury backs,
And the younglettes were glad that they were safe and sound,
As the returned to Thistledown Town deep in the woods,
They flew back to their mother who was waiting on the ground.
The Pixilettes hugged their mother with love so very tight,
And the girls told the tale of all they had heard and seen,
Safe after their adventures in the giant human town,
Henriella and Robertina explained that the humans weren't mean.
The younglettes told mother about the big people's home,
And about how they now know the people were good and kind,
They weren't what the Pixilettes thought, and so it just goes to show,
You should get to know someone before you make up your mind.

Poorly Alistair Bear

Alistair was feeling like a very poorly little bear,
Who really needed some tender loving care.
He went to bear hospital to see Doctor Clairebear,
And to rest in the comfy bed and arm soft chair.

At hospital Nursebear Sair looked after him well,
and put a plaster on his arm from where he fell.
Doctor Clairebear gave him medicine and an injection as well,
She smiled "In no time Alistair, we'll have you feeling swell."

Alistair snuggled in bed to rest like he should,
He drank all his juice and ate as much as he could.
He listened to the doctors and nurses who were all very good,
And Alastair took all his tablets like a good bear would.

Now Doctor Clairebear said Alistair could go home,
But he needed his Daddy so he wasn't alone.
Alistair was so so brave and he tried not to moan,
He read some books in bed and called his friends on the phone.

With a few days rest and cuddles from Dad,
Soon Alistair thought he didn't feel too bad.
He remembered the hospital and the medicine he had,
Yes, for everyone's kindness he would forever be glad.

Now Alistair wants to be a Nursebear when he grows up,
To look after poorly bears who are down on their luck.
He'll take good care of his patients and never give up,
Ready at bear hospital anytime where the doors never shut.

Who Lives At The South Pole?

I bet you all know who lives at the North Pole,
Yes, I'm sure that's a story you've always been told,
But the South Pole, do you know who lives there?
Nope, because that secret is so very very old.

I'll tell you, for once I did actually meet her,
When I was meant to be quiet and asleep,
Yes, I saw her there one dark winters night,
From under the covers, I did silently peep.

She came to collect what I had left under my pillow,
Travelling from the South Pole all the way to my bed,
You see I've been expecting to see her, so it wasn't a fright.
As she came to leave me a coin for my lost tooth instead.

I watched quietly and let her do her work,
And I was truly amazed at the sight,
But then she sighed with sadness,
And cried she because she had a bad night.

I asked her whatever was the matter,
And told her not to be sad,
You know that when a problem is shared,
It is then never half as bad.

Through a sniffle and a tear, she whispered to me,
About how hard she worked each and every night,
And yet nobody even knew where she lived,
Oh my, how could that ever be right.

Then suddenly I had a crazy idea,
Maybe she should write Santa a list,
She could tell him everything she needs,

Then maybe he can help with her wish.

"Thank you my dear!" she cried,
And off she travelled home,
All the way to the South Pole,
Where she wouldn't be alone.

At the grand and white sparkly castle,
You go through big gates to get in,
And when you finally get there,
You'll be greeted by the chief penguin!

The South Pole is where she stores the teeth,
With the help of her gentle penguin hoard,
They are busy all through the year,
There's no time at all to get bored.

That Christmas Eve she tucked away her letter,
And went hopelessly off to bed,
But Chief Penguin read the letter,
And posted it off with magic dust instead.

For all her years of hard work,
And time spend helping everyone else,
This was the only thing,
That she'd truly wanted for herself.

The penguins told her she made a difference,
Although she never got to see it,
And when she was tired from working all year,
It became harder to believe it.
But on that morning it happened,
She couldn't believe what she had seen,
After all these long years working hard,
For her now Santa had finally been.

The penguins all smiled looking glad,
As she opened her present with glee,
It was some sort of magical globe,
Whatever could this thing be?

Round and crystal with a brass stand,
"Its a Wonderglobe" Chief Penguin said,
"So you can see all the happy children,
As they wake up to find your coin in their bed"

"Its perfect!!" she said grinning widely,
And hugged the globe so very tight,
She'd finally be able to see the joy,
That she brought to children after each night.

The penguins all gather close around,
And hugged this kind-hearted soul,
Now the penguins and the Tooth Fairy,
Were a happy family at the South Pole.

My Dear Teacher

My teacher really was the best teacher in the whole school,
The children all loved her and thought she was so cool.
She helps them to learn new things and follow the rules,
And my teacher was the funniest person at the school.
At story time my teacher always read the very best books,
She made a journey of their learning with the pictures she took.
With the stunning starts to topics all the children were hooked,
And some nights she worked late, for as long as it took.
But the best thing about my teacher was how kind she would be,
She has plasters ready if any children bump their knee.
And a massive hug for little ones who are missing anybody,
Yes my teacher always has a "Good morning" and smile for me.
So thank you for this year of learning and all you have done,
We've enjoyed the plays, sports days and picnics in the sun.
My dear teacher you truly are very special and lots of fun,
I will miss you so much now my school journey moves on.
(But perhaps you can come back to teach me again another year on!)

Milton Keynes UK
Ingram Content Group UK Ltd.
UKHW022050040124
435404UK00016B/412